Dear, Black Girl. Please remember that you are all of the things in this book and MORE. You are YOU and no one can take that from you. I hope you enjoy!

Love your friend and Author,

-Eboni Dockery

This book belongs to the AMAZING:

_____

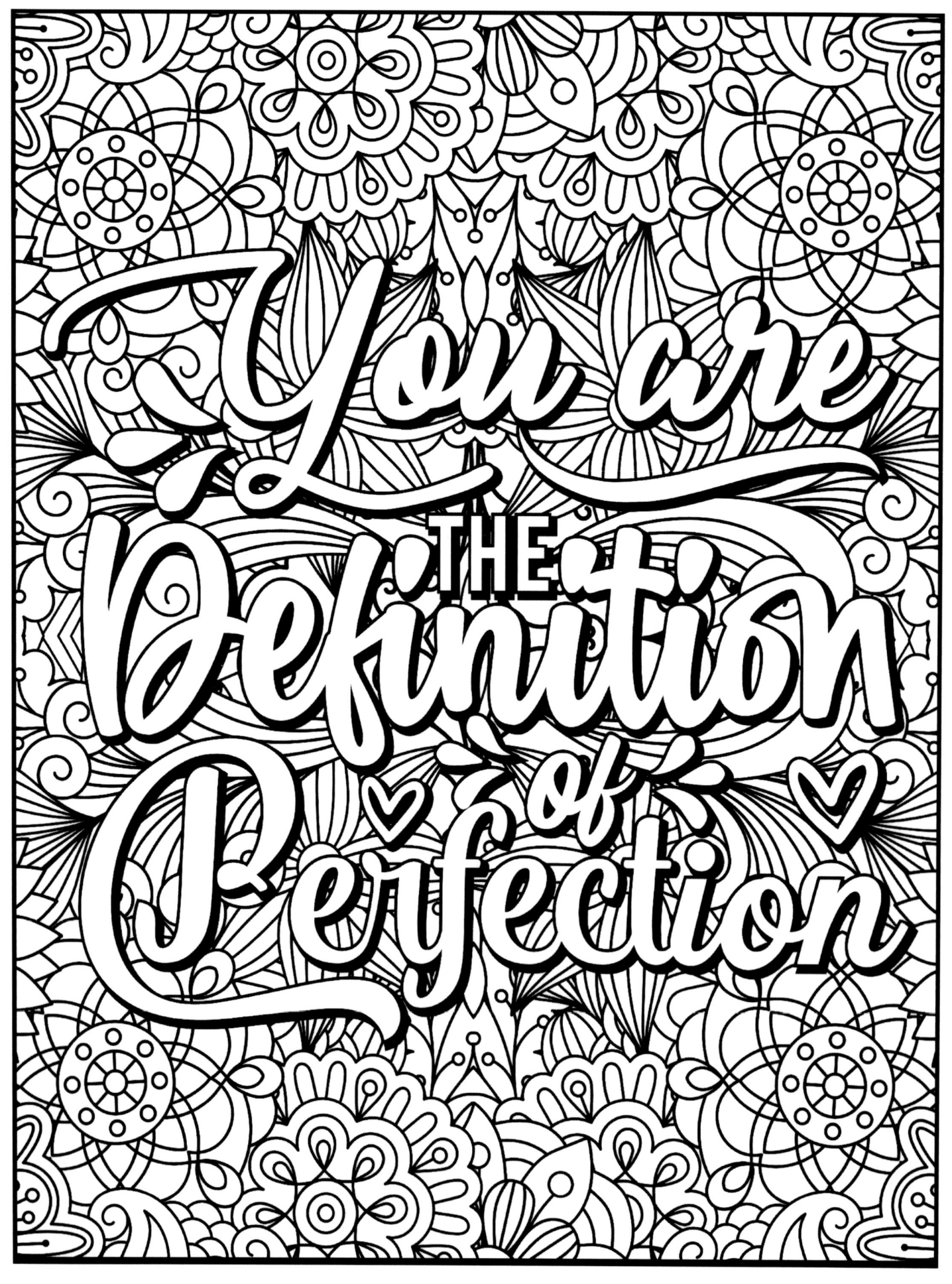

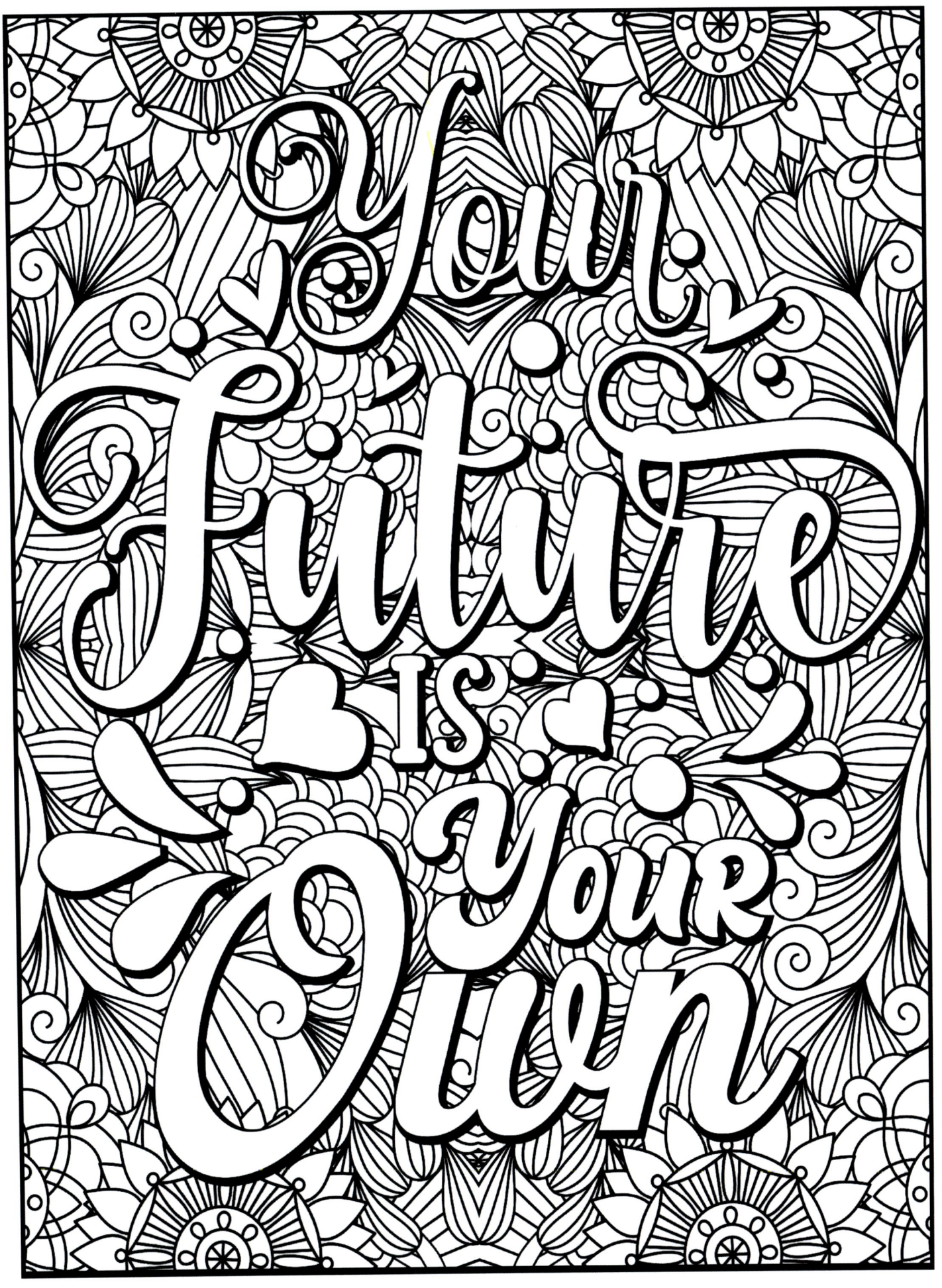

Made in the USA
Middletown, DE
03 December 2023